Forward
Tracking The Holy Spirit
By Krystal Klear

Dedicated to an awesome God, the Father; the Son and the Holy Spirit. (H.S.)

These modern parables are seeds of truth, planted by reading and passed on, to reveal in simple language, answers to what seems to be difficult to understand.

Having written this book to the specifications given me surpasses any imagination I could dream up.

I have been honored beyond belief to be made aware of my personal relationship with Jesus and have it used in this manner. However the names have been changed for obvious reasons.

This is a work of fiction but the events really happened.

A miracle:
Rob, my nay saying husband, has typed every word. Where I found errors, rearranged sentences or added a thought he willingly, patiently redid the typing.

He's a keeper.

I am the daughter of the "I Am"

Table of Contents
H.S.(Holy Spirit)

Pg. 1   The Oil Drum Boat
            H.S.   Rescue's- - -Sent Aunt Eve

Pg. 3   Stony Point
            H.S.   Protects- - -Sent Grandpa Person

Pg. 5   Winter Rescue
            H.S.   Rescue's- - -Sent Ron's Cousin

Pg. 6   Le Bully
            H.S.   Protects, Corrects- - -
                       Sent Brother Don

Pg. 8   Unbelievable Tragedy
            H.S.   Observes

Pg. 10   The Move
            H.S.   Observes, Involved

Pg. 11   The Test
            H.S.   On Hold

Pg. 12   Angel's Unaware
            H.S.   Super Natural Engineering- - -
                       Sent Host of Heaven

Pg. 14   Cat & The Canary
            H.S.   Power of Prayer Comforts- - -
                       Sent Anna

Pg. 16   Mindy
            H.S.   Under Cover Agent- - -
                       Sent Elleen

Table of Contents (cont.)

Pg. 19		A Smile Draped The Heaven's
	H.S.	Communicates-- Personal Contact
Pg. 20		Fire Engine Rescue
	H.S.	Rescue's
Pg. 22		A Soft Answer
	H.S.	Involved Personally
Pg. 24		No Miracle
	H.S.	Prayer Answered--- His Name is John
Pg. 27		Henry Who?
	H.S.	Comfort's, Compassion
Pg. 29		From Pew To Pulpit
	H.S.	Agrees with Prayer & Answers
Pg. 31		Wake Up Call
	H.S.	Is Grieved
Pg. 34		Beware Of Visitor's Bearing Gifts
	H.S.	Not Involved
Pg. 35		Birthday Party
	H.S.	Allowed Deception
Pg. 36		Getting Back On Track
	H.S.	Involved
Pg. 37		God's Perfect Timing
	Bible	Matt. 15:10, 18 & 19

Table of Contents (cont.)

Pg. 39   What Vision? This Vision?
        Bible   Matt. 25: 1 - 13

Pg. 41   Fatal Fall
        H,S.   Revealed- - - God's sense of Humor

              And The Point Is- - - -Krystal Klear

Tracking the Holy Spirit
by Krystal Klear

The Oil Drum Boat

Here it is at last a bright sunny day. School Is out and I beat my older brother, Don, home. This means his boat is available and I can get a ride in it. Ronnie Hart, our next door neighbor, sees me pushing the boat toward the creek and want's a ride also. "You can't come", I told him (3 times) but he just jumped in.

The boat wasn't very big. Don found it somewhere. It was an oil drum cut in half and he put a board across the middle for a seat. Our ride didn't last very long because Ronnie kept rocking the boat. I said, "stop that or I'm going to fall in." Again he wouldn't listen and I fell in. I came up under the boat. By now all of the noise we were making was heard by Aunt Eve, who lived at the point where I fell in.

Nowhere could I get out of the water except to climb up the wall made of slag pieces on her land. The wall was eight (8) feet high. I was eight (8) years old and small for my age. Aunt Eve said, "Elleen come up here." I remember looking up at her and I thought that I could climb that wall---and I did! Aunt Eve reached down as far as she could and pulled me up to safety.

My new dress that I was wearing had a tear in it. Also I smelled like that rat infested Ecorse Creek. When I reached home, I heard those familiar words from my Mom, "Downstairs. Get into the laundry tub".

I don't know whatever happened to the boat or to Ronnie and I don't recall hearing any discussion or receiving any punishment from my parents. Maybe they were glad to have me safe and sound, Do you think? I sure felt bad about my dress.

Stony Point

Stony Point was a favorite place for Mom and Dad to take us for a Sunday afternoon of swimming and picnicking. We stayed at Uncle Art and Aunt Hazel's cottage. It was here Aunt Hazel served us fried green tomatoes for dinner besides a lunch fit for a king.

The beach was about three (3) blocks from the cottage. I decided to go for a swim alone. I could do this because I was big enough. I was six (6).

There it is, the water, and I ran into it. It was nice and warm but when I looked down where my foot was hurting the water was red. I backed out of the water and looking at my foot I saw blood. Someone had thrown a broken Coke bottle in the water and I stepped on it.

Now I am walking on my heel and bleeding every step of the way to go to my dad. Passing cottages and crying caught the attention of a man on a porch who was watching me struggle along. He came to me and seeing my problem asked me if I knew where I lived and what happened. I said. "yes!". I had walked one half of a block and needed to go another two and a half blocks. The man picked me up and carried me to my parents. I just knew he was a grandpa. Grandpa's help you.

My Mom wanted to take me to a doctor but Dad, being a farm boy, said, " Just bind the cut toe together. It will heal." Dad was right. The one toe that was cut nearly in half did heal.

That particular day was so hot, I wondered why that man was out on his porch. No one else was out on their porches. It's a sure thing that I needed him. The sun was beating down on the porches on that side of the street where the man had been sitting He had long pants on not even shorts for such a hot day.

Having cut my toe was bad but what could have been worse. I could have drowned. No one knew where I was.

Winter Rescue

It's a cold Sunday afternoon and Ron's cousin, a hockey player, is coming out to practice on the ice. Ron and I are going to skate there too. When we arrived there, his cousin was already playing hockey. So Ron and I just skated around.

Just as unpredictable as ice can be, I hit a weak spot and the ice gave way under me. Now I'm in the water and I can't get out. Every attempt I make to pull myself out, the ice keeps giving way. Ronnie can't help. If he tried he would fall in also. He skated over to his cousin who came and saw I was in big trouble. He approached but knew the ice would not hold him either, He was big. He called out to me to watch as he skated toward me and at the right time reach up my arms and as he flew over me he grabbed my arms. We landed on safe ice.

I went home all wet again. Recalling this, I'm thinking Ronnie made up for the time he caused me to fall out of my brother's boat.

Perhaps I was ten (10) years old when this happened.

Le Bully

During the summer months when school was out at Raupp School, where we attended in Lincoln Park, a Craft program was offered. Mrs. Kennedy was in charge and I liked making the different projects.

On a particular day upon leaving the rest room an overweight, bigger than me, girl said she was going to beat me up and for no reason. Yes I was scared. When leaving the building I made sure that I walked close behind Mrs. Kennedy as that girl was closing in on me.

Mrs. Kennedy drove off in her car and I headed for home running. A block and a half later, I was at my front yard and right behind me was that bully. How Don, my brother, happened to be right there I'll never know. I ran up to him telling him, "She's gonna beat me up." Immediately he took over and told her, "You get your fat ass out of here or I'll beat the shit out of you. And leave my sister alone." Little did I know that some ten years later Don would marry Doris Monroe whose best friend was the fat ass.

I was impressed with the power that swearing had and my brother's and I used it routinely when we were together. But we never swore where our parents were. Somehow you knew not to. Besides they never did swear.

For the first time my brother's and I bonded but not for long as the swearing from me was stopped unexpectedly and abruptly. I was twelve and on my way to school when from within me a voice thundered, "You sound terrible." I was practicing swearing. I did - - I know I did. I stopped swearing right then. Now the voice was in front of me, talking to me as I walked along and I accepted Jesus as my Lord and Saviour right then.

There was no one walking with me. This was nothing amazing or fantastic to me I knew God could do anything he chooses. Anyway I was 12 now and my every Saturday for two years spent in Catechism would teach me so much more for a future that would include Jesus in my life but not yet.

Unbelievable Tragedy

On July 26, 1961 tragedy struck my brother's home and family. He and his wife and 5 children drove to Oscoda to vacation. They rented a cabin from friends whom they knew. The cabin was built to keep out the cold air. They called this method tongue and groove. The cabin also had a Servel refrigerator which emitted gas. The refrigerator was not keeping the food cold enough, so my brother lowered its temperature.

The next morning the children were not outSide and by noon the owners of the cabin went to See why. They found them all overcome by gas. The Parent's and Gary lived but Harold (12), Nancy (10), Cathy (8) and Julie (14mo's) had died. All of Lincoln Park came to the viewing and to the funeral. At least it seemed that way.

Before this and for some time this marriage had been in trouble and now a deluge of circumstances added to it. There was a divorce leaving Gary with his father but no one to take care of Gary during the time his dad worked. The father needed someone to take care of Gary. Being aware of this, I talked to my then husband, Bob, sighting the fact that Gary could be neglected or with a non-Christian.

And what about the love that Gary needed. Also, This could just be a job for someone else. Bob told me, "If that's what you want to do, we'll do it." And that's what I wanted, to raise Gary.

Not having children of my own and Gary was number five for my sister-in-law. She was saddened by remarks being made about her having another baby. We were talking in the garden at her home in Lincoln Park and I told her, "You have this baby for me." She said she would. I know she felt better.

The first week in February my brother came to my house asking me to go with him to the hospital. The baby was coming home. They never had me come when the other babies were born. I waited in the car at the hospital for them to come out. When they did, I got out of the car to see the baby. Then my sister-in-law handed him to me. He was beautiful and perfect. I didn't know then that I would be raising Gary.

For a short time we lived with Henry and Gary at their house but this was just not working. A close friend of the family told Bob that I needed my own home. So we drove around looking for a house but Bob drove out in the country which just wouldn't do. It was desolate for me - - no neighbors.

The Move

I had to be near my brother, Don, that's all I knew. I felt, not way out in the country where Bob was taking me to find a house. I remembered a couple that had visited Don and Toots, while we were there. They said they were going to sell their house. They lived at the end of the street where Don lived in Romulus. I remembered this as we drove past their house going to see my brother. So I pleaded with Bob to turn around and ask them to sell us their house. He said, "They won't sell their house!" He didn't want to but he did turn around. I stayed in the car. When he returned he said, "They sold us their house!"

I had been asking God to heal me and I promised to help anyone that felt as I did. In our new home, being near my brother, I felt safe. It would be sometime before being better was my condition having to deal with anxiety 24/7. Elavil and Triavil were my companions from my doctor.

The Test

Within the first month I learned of Henrietta. She was Don's neighbor and living a nervous breakdown for years. It registered. I knew how she felt. On a certain morning, walking home from a visit with my sister-in-law, a neighbor had come to her mail box just as I got there. She said, "You're Don's sister, aren't you?" I said, "Yes." She said, "I'm having a nervous breakdown." She elaborated until my own anxiety had me tell her, "I'll come back tomorrow", and I hurried home.

My promise to help those who felt as I do is right here where I moved. Now what? I can't do this. Not yet, I moaned. Time went by and I heard Henrietta's husband was thinking of putting her away, which means I cannot keep my promise. Now What? I hurried up the street to Henrietta's house. She answered my knock at the front door. They use the back door. Seeing me she said, "You're Don's sister!" I said, "Yes, I've come to help you," She said. "No one knows how I feel!" I said, "Yes, I do." And I told her how I felt. She hugged me and we cried.

From this day on, I would walk to Anna's, the other lady on our street having a breakdown, get her and we would both go to Henrietta's. Every story should have a happy ending and Henrietta rallied for a time but she did die.

Angel's Unaware

Anna and I continued being friends, really good friends. How many friends would, at midnight, take you to the store to get a cigar for your sick husband who just wished he had a cigar. He was incapacitated due to Pagets' disease. His desire for a Corona could have been his dying wish or ours. It was winter and this particular night it began to rain on the already ice packed streets. We realized this but went anyway, thinking, to take the back roads would be better than the highway.

It was bad and there were no houses with lights on as we crawled along. Suddenly we were hit from behind, we thought. But there were no cars behind us and now we were sliding dangerously back and forth on this side road. Anna was driving really well. We were laughing and sailing along just having fun until the car flipped over the 3ft ditch landing on an iron sign post in the middle of someone's yard.

The snow was knee deep. Now what to do? It just happened the house, in the yard where we landed, was lit up. I told Anna to do her thing and I would go and ask for help. Anna's thing was, being a pentacostal believer, so praying was like now. There was a truck in the drive way and that looked like the answer. I knocked on the door and a man answered with his bottle of beer in hand.

He saw our car and right away knew I would ask for help to use his truck. His answer was the truck doesn't run.

I turned to walk away and saw six men at the car, three on each side. I hurried out to stand on that iron post to help somehow and as they lifted the car I was thrown into a snow pile. Now, the man in the house came to help. One of the men picked me up saying,"There you are young lady," and he was gone. They all were gone leaving us with questions like, "Where did they come from?" and," How did they get the car over a three foot ditch?"

They put the car in the direction we would be going and the biggest realization was they had no winter clothes on. They were dressed for spring. We did get the cigar and had a tale to tell to go with it. Oh yes! We took the express way home.

Cat & The Canary

Everything is better now that we are in our own home.

On a certain day preparing supper for Bob and Gary I happened to look out the back yard window and observed the cutest little cat sitting patiently waiting for the big cats to finish eating and hopefully leave her some.

She licked at the empty plate and left. This touched my heart and I had to put out enough food for her too. She was calico in color, couldn't have been six weeks old and I determined to make her mine.

Every night I would put her food in the front yard where she crossed to come and eat, gradually moving it closer to the porch where I intended to be. The evening came when she saw me and her food. She paced back and forth and back and forth until I left.

The time came when I didn't leave and I had a long pincher that had her meat on it. If she wanted it she had to come and eat it off the pincher.

Two weeks this went on and I had the pincher but she could come for her food in her plate now. When she did I stroked her gently with the pincher.

This went on for a time and finally I could touch her and then pet her and the best day came when I could pick her up. She would come running at supper time and it was great since my husband had told me "you'll never tame that cat. It's wild."

For some reason birds' would fly into our windows with a bang. A canary hit it so hard he killed himself. Bob buried it by the huge tree in our back yard. About this time the little kitty came to eat but she was real sick. We took her to the Vet who helped her but she insisted on going out and every time she came home she was sick. The last time she crawled to me and died at my feet.

You know how some people are----they take these things so seriously-----well I did. I fell apart crying, crying and crying. My mother was here. Her comment was, "How long are you going to hold that cat? It is dead !" I had worked so hard to have her.

Anna stopped in. It was evening and Bob had buried the cat with the canary under the same tree. Anna took over putting me to bed, prayed for me and stroked my brow. I did sleep and I saw the cat. I am calling her. I know she'll come but she's chasing something up that tree where they were buried and they're moving fast. Now I see what she is after. It's the little canary and now they're into the clouds. I awake full of joy.

Thank you Anna for your prayers. Thank You Lord for sending Anna.

Mindy

Money can always be a problem when you need more and Anna was on her way to accept a part time job caring for Dorothy, who had been bed ridden for some sixteen years. I rode along. We entered the driveway where Dorothy's husband, Bill, had just returned home from work. Anna and Bill talked but she decided not to take the job.

The job was a matter of getting breakfast for Dorothy and to help her with the bed pan. Now that I am older I realize she could have gotten to the bath room as easily as she did breakfast, using her walker.

Oh! Well---so much for hind sight. While fixing Dorothy's breakfast I would listen to Christian radio. At her first breakfast I told her I would be quiet while she prayed. She said, "You pray Elleen." I did and she ate. Two days later Dorothy informed me she had a daughter that tried to force religion down her throat and Dorothy wants none of it. I apologized and turned off the radio during her breakfast.

Dorothy had two dogs. One was obviously sick. I was concerned because I had my little dog, Missy, with me and that she might catch something made me anxious. I asked Dorothy when she was going to take Mindy to the doctor. "Bill will take her. I'll tell him", she said.

The next day at work Dorothy told me Bill took Mindy to the doctor but did not get the medicine. It wasn't what he wanted and he had no way of getting it. Mindy had distemper. Which is considered a non-curable illness and other dogs could catch it.

Dorothy said, "Mindy is going to die", I said, "Dorothy maybe I could get that medicine." She said, "Elleen, Bill will pay you. You get that medicine."

Mindy was Dorothy's companion well into the night when Bill would come home after drinking. I had a plan and had Bob take me to the veterinarian where we go. Bill used the same vet. I went in and explained to them that my husband had changed his mind and he will take the medicine. I told them I was Dorothy---Bill's wife. I got the medicine.

The next day I didn't even get to close the door before Dorothy was asking if I got the medicine. I replied in the affirmative. But now I needed a request from Dorothy. I said, "I need to lay my hands on Mindy every day and pray." Dorothy replied, "Elleen pray for my Mindy." And so it was. After I'd pray Dorothy would say, "Amen", too.

Dorothy was happy but now to get Mindy to take the medicine. She would not. My strong husband could not get her jaws open. Now what??? I crushed the pill and mixed the powder into tuna fish oil. Then with an atomizer I squirted the mixture into the side of her mouth. It worked.

Morning and evening we went to give Mindy her medicine. The days past---18-19-20-21 and on the 22nd day I heard a dog bark. Until now there was no response. I ran in to Dorothy and said, "Was that Mindy?" She said, "Yes" and we both cried and watched Mindy jump off of the bed and go to her dish where Bill had her beer.

We took Mindy to the vet to have her checked. He saw us coming and he ran from us saying he wouldn't touch Mindy because she's too sick. Unbelievable but true.

One week after Mindy recovered Dorothy was eating her breakfast and was telling me she was going to be baptized. Oh I said, "That's good. When are you going to do this?" "Next Saturday", she said. I said, "Who is going to do this?" "Your minister", she replied "You call him."

Remember Dorothy has not been out of her house in sixteen years. So this seems like it could happen. I called my minister, Pastor Schellhase, at that time and he did come.

It was a beautiful sunny afternoon. Dorothy was wheeled out into her back yard and then Pastor asked her why she wanted to be baptized. Her answer, "Because God healed my Mindy." Oh! I thought, wrong answer but it wasn't because Dorothy recognized God.

The eyes of the blind were opened.

A Smile Draped The Heaven's

Shortly after this my Bob's illness, Paget's disease, grew worse and he did die. But before this and while he was still working we went to bed early one evening. During the early hours of the morning I was hearing someone talking to me while I slept. Caution welled up inside me and I said, "Are you my Lord and Savior or Satan? If Satan get away from me in the name of Jesus."

With that I saw myself looking out my bedroom window where a Smile draped the heaven's. I had pleased God but I was in bed at the same time. Now God is leaving me and I want to go with him. The peace that passes all understanding is where he is and quiet joy filled my soul. This memory lingers on to this day.

Fire Engine Rescue

It's picnic time in Belleville and the Chiropractor in town is affording his patients a wonderful fun time and food at Van Buren park. Even a fire engine is here for everyone to inspect.

At this time I am not walking well not having made arrangements for hip surgery yet. However Rob remembers this area from his childhood and wants Elizabeth, our friend, and me to walk to the water and show us what he would like us to see. "It's not far," he says. But it was. When we finally saw the water and the view which was worth seeing I had no strength to walk back down the road and up a hill.

To top it off, it was isolated and no one was coming or going. But there was an old picnic table a few feet away and I went over and sat on it saying, "I'm not leaving here till my ride come's." Elizabeth said, "What ride?" I thought, "Is she kidding?" So I said, "A fire engine."

There was no more conversation while we waited and rested. In the distance, coming down the road, we could hear a motorized something approaching. We couldn't see anything due to the over growth. Then in plain sight here comes a fire engine. I waved and ran to them to stop. They did and I asked them if we could have a ride. The answer was yes. By now Rob and Elizabeth were here and we stepped onto the running board to ride back to the picnic area.

The firemen grinned and said, "Open the door and get in." Oh! I didn't know. There was a couch inside. The firemen drove us to our car. As we passed the picnic area the fire engine we thought had come to rescue us was still parked there. These firemen were from Ypsilanti and were looking for a place to turn around. They just happened to drive to this isolated area. Were we fortunate or what?

A Soft Answer

We had been blessed some 24 years to have a Director of Music at St. Paul's Lutheran Church in Dearborn for this length of time. Although at times his patience wore thin with displeasure when the many times of instruction were just ignored.

Added expectations and more commitment for his time helped bring his demeanor to the boiling point. And so it happened, after many warnings, he picked a person to crash on. He exploded and I was the lucky choice in a tirade that had the choir members gasping. Glaring at me, he said, "Elleen I am the choir director. Not you!"

You see we are not to speak at rehearsals'. The gal next to me, coming in late, asked me which piece of music we were to sing. I told her and he took this as defiance. I tried to explain to no avail, which was obvious, but then, why I don't know, I put my arm around her and looking at him I said, "But I love her!" I really didn't know her. He backed off and returned to directing.

For sure no one expected me to come again To rehearsal but this is God's house. I am committed to return to the Lord the singing voice he gave me. Besides I was fine, just fine afterwards, as I felt no upset at all. I was aware that there was a weight on my chest like when you ride in a crowded elevator and the person in front of you must lean on you.

I was sure the Shield of Faith was what had protected me and I was overjoyed telling Rob this at home. At this precise moment, while looking up at Rob, I saw Jesus arm from shoulder to hand covering my heart. His robe was the whitest white and his hand was the color of bronze. I realized I had been allowed the great privilege of having a personal relationship with Jesus.

None of this seemed strange. Why would it? Had I not been learning to lean on Jesus as a child. Executing it seriously would be in my future and hind sight would be the eye opener.

No Miracle

In the year 2000 we traveled to Philadelphia and New Jersey with a young Intern Pastor. He had stored his belongings there until he was established permanently at which time he would return to get them. He was planning to rent a U-haul truck to do this but we had a utility van available. So we all traveled together to get his things.

It was in New Jersey where we were hit by a huge garbage truck. Our van was totaled and our friend had to rent a truck to get his belongings back to Dearborn, MI. Neither he nor Rob, my husband, were injured while I had 8 vertebrae out of line, a black eye and one arm 3 times its size having been trapped beneath the driver's seat. Yes, I was riding on the back seat.

It took the jaws-of-life to free me. However had I not been trapped this way I could easily have died. After this, Osteoporosis gradually crept into my hips. Needing hip replacements became necessary but who and how to choose a surgeon was a big problem.

Many friends offered their doctor and I did go To Botsford hospital where a doctor there told me to have his mentor do the surgery as the condition of my hips was too bad. Now what? The word mentor wasn't clear to me and I'm back to mentally struggling. What to do? How do I choose?

Since praying for a miracle, which wasn't happening and I need direction, I'll ask God to send someone right in my face. So, without a doubt, I'll know what to do. This was Saturday night and I dreamed. Sunday morning, upon waking, I related the dream I had to Rob.

The dream: I was outside Christ Lutheran Church in Detroit, on Scotten and Wolf streets, where I attended until I was 18. Just before going in, I see a young man hesitating. So I invited him to come in. I went in alone but as I went up the steps, inside I see my Mother and Father folding bulletins at a table, just as they used to do. They were both in their 30's. Mom had her dark hair and lost weight and Dad was himself. They had both died (Dad in '71 and Mom in '88). The year I'm writing about is 2003.

Looking into the Church I see the young man from outside the Church sitting in a pew evidently with his family. I realized he needed no invitation from me to come in. The dream ends here as Rob woke me up to get ready for church. It pleased me to see my Mom and Dad. A good feeling.

We have coffee hour before church service and I was settled in my wheeler munching on coffee cake, etc. When I looked up a tall young man, new I thought, came for coffee hour. I asked him to come and sing in our choir. He rattled off about a too busy life but now he was in front of me asking why I was not walking.

My short answer, "I just don't know how to choose a doctor!" His response was, "I am going to help you, I am going to help you!." I was now in tears. His tone of voice is so positive and I'm so in need of this.

His name is John and he explains his position in pharmacies and then asks what we have done so far. I relate the Botsford Hospital report to him. I am to go to the Mentor for surgery which had John respond, "You go to the Mentor. He is the teacher of the surgeon's." John is very tall so he has kneeled in front of me to talk at which time I am seeing the young man in my dream. The color of his hair, his haircut, the clothes he was wearing were the same and his family attends our church as does he.

We talked further and he reminded me that I taught him to sing in vacation bible school years ago. He was little then. Now he is 6'2". We laughed. Here is an immediate answer to my prayer and such gratitude to have the Holy Spirit use John Mohler. From now on I will make sure that what I ask of God will be what he wants me to ask.

Henry Who?

Both surgeries have been successful but after the second surgery, after recovery, I was very, very weak. Getting out of bed to go to the bath room was unreal effort. I really did not want to bother the nurses because they insisted I was to get up without any assistance.

It seems that when you are at your lowest and reach out to God, He comes through. I really needed help again. This time a young man about 30ish came. I told him my woeful story. Without a word he picked me up like a child and placed me on the floor. I went about my business and returned at which time he picked me up and put me back to bed.

The second and third day he always came when I rang for help. I tried to engage him in conversation like, "What is your name?". He responded, "Henry", to which I replied that, " I had an older brother named Henry. He died 4 years ago." There was no more conversation as I volunteered once, "I think I'll take you home with me!" His no response clued me in that he likes it like that. I did thank him sincerely each time he helped.

Six weeks later we would learn more about Henry as I had a doctor's appointment. We wanted to thank Henry by giving him a gift certificate. We told the doctor about this and he told us to go to the floor where I was a patient. We did and learned from the head nurse that they never had a Henry working there. She sent us to the employment office down stairs assuring us they would know. Here we were told the same thing. They never employed a Henry.

Which tells me - - - The Father to whom I prayed and the Son Jesus, who is the mediator, said he would send the Comforter when he left. This promise he kept when Henry appeared.

From Pew to Pulpit

Sunday mornings would find us seated in the front pew at St. Paul's Lutheran Church in Dearborn. This was due to the fact that the osteoporosis in my hips being so painful, it was easier to receive Holy Communion.

This particular Sunday we arrived early and I was in my pew. No one else was in the church yet. A perfect setting to talk to Jesus as his life size statue encourages us to recall he gave his life for us sinners. He was sinless and to this day will not be where evil is.

Anyway, being full of gratitude for all he has done for me, I am telling him, "If there was anything I could do to please him, I would." The assistant minister is now in the Altar area arranging prayers and checking that the epistle's in the Bible are correct for this Sunday. I am watching her and the Lord whispered to me two words, "Do this!".
"You mean Lay Assistant Minister?" I asked. "Do this!" he repeated. "Oh! I can't do that", I said.

Well, the Church service concluded and we went home. Imagine promising to do anything to please God and he finds something. Wouldn't you know. Now what? I'll tell you what- -- - a week long guilt trip was my due.

The following two Sunday's in church again I still did not volunteer to be a Lay Assistant Minister. The same guilt trip plagued me and I had to do something. So I figured I'd just tell him I'd do it and he would leave me alone. Immediately I knew he knows our every thought.

I found the Lay Assistant Minister coordinator and volunteered. She was pleased. This was a training on the job deal. Everything went fine, especially my interpretation of the reading of the Epistle's.

Communion went well and now it was time to give Pastor the bread and wine and then he serves them to me. I guess I was a little nervous. When he gave me the wafer, I put it into my mouth - - - oops, the wafer is dipped into the wine then into the mouth. Immediately I took the wafer out of my mouth, dipped it into the wine and put it back into my mouth.

After the service I said to Pastor Borman, "That wasn't so good was it?". He replied, "That was Pretty bad".

Time has gone by and I can tell you as always God knows what he is asking. He created me so he knew my ability when I didn't. What about trusting God? I didn't did I?

Wake Up Call

Remember in High School the fun you had splitting up couples. My question - - "Is it that much fun now?" Every day we talked. It was my morning call to you as when we first met you told me everyone calls you. You don't call anyone, so I thought that's fine, I get to call when I choose.

Our friendship bloomed. It was good. We agreed we were "forever friends" and you had my back. Somehow the "forever" became, you would not take my phone calls after only one year. I called three times. The last time the phone was answered by your daughter who said what you told her to say from the background, "Tell her I'm alright."

I was concerned. I was never to hear from you again but would see you among the friends when no conversation could take place. Naturally I would search my brain to figure out the why of this.

The last time we were together was August of 2009. We were talking about September's birthday party and who the special guest would be. I had decided. This was up to me.

Several times your son-in-law and my nephew had bonded talking about sports cars as Clark had one and Craig knew everything about cars. When first they met Clark was blind due to diabetes. He had two prosthesis, a triple bypass surgery, a kidney given to him and a new pancreas. And in their world he could at least relate verbally. Talking with Craig made his day in his dark world but now Clark has sight in one eye having had a cataract removed.

This would be the perfect guest and Clark would see Craig. They would talk. You said, "He won't come!" I said I can invite them anyway as his wife would be invited as well and you repeated, "He won't come!" I didn't need to ask why. The answer would have nothing to do with me. "I'll just send an invitation." No more was said. We're talking about 50 year olds who can refuse if they make the choice. Which would be fine but they have to have the choice. Here is when the phone calls I made would not be answered. Not talking to me - - - how could I invite your son-in-law, Craig?

You came to Clark's party knowing you stopped me from inviting Craig but you really like Clark! Right? When we celebrated your birthday and your brother came to surprise you. I let no one spoil your surprise. You were so-o-o pleased he came.

Where is this going now?! Not to go on my own determination, it's time to enlist elder help, meaning wise council. This we found offered in one sentence. "This is not your friend!" What about being discerning, as spoken in the word. I wasn't was I? Face value won out.

Beware of Visitor's Bearing Gifts

October seemed to fly by. It's time to plan for a very special birthday in November. Francine will be 90 years old. She can't believe it herself. There was little for me to do as Coral Ford, Francine's daughter, requested she be allowed to bring the cake and would I tell her how many to expect. For the life long friends who have been so thoughtful to her mother she would like to buy their dinners. There are 5 of us. Not a problem.

Invitation letters were sent out requesting an "R.S.V.P." response. The number was forwarded to Coral. Mona called 3 times telling us she had church and could not come. These messages were on our phone's answering tape.

The Saturday before the party Francine had three unexpected visitors, Johanna, Nora Dee and Mona. They had presents for Francine telling her they would not be coming to her party because they were not invited. Fracine knew this was not true but the unexpected surprise left her speechless. She felt obligated to invite them to her party. She added her daughter was buying the dinners. She just could not think, to which Mona said, "We coming to your party, we coming to your party."

Birthday Party

Guests are arriving and on time including the three Saturday night unexpected visitor's. My surprise showed on my face and the reaction I received was, "They have a personal invitation." He was angry with me. I learned later what they had done. Apparently the remark I received is because he was led to believe I had slighted them. He believes this and he knows me so well.

The party went off without a hitch. Francine wore the birthday Crown. We sang, "Bless our friends, bless our food. Come oh Lord and sit with us. May our talk glow with peace," etc. Coral knew before I did what happened when I came to apologize to her. She was gracious telling me it was alright.

In all our years together nothing like this occurred. Beware of those who cause division.

Getting Back On Track

Tracking the Holy Spirit culminates when a friend, at the senior center, overheard what was being said about me and Francine. Untrue implications from the same false friends from the birthday party. She innocently related what she heard, then overnight a conscience attack made her feel guilty and the next day she apologized.

I forgave her immediately. It wasn't her fault. Friendly chatter was the problem, for want of a better word. I turned to walk away and saw the words on her husband's shirt. In bold print it read, "God is Wise." I said to them, "God knows how to let us know he is involved!" Awesome!

Two days later her husband died.
God's Perfect Timing.

God's Perfect Timing

This perfect timing led me to read Glenna Henderson's book, "My name is Legion."

The senior center was busy with people walking the halls, playing cards, playing pool, enjoying country western music, the quilting class, the painting class, the German class, the Lively Singers, the Music Maker's and one little 97 year old lady quietly reading her book, seated in the hallway. As I passed by, I greeted her and asked her what she was reading, to which she responded, "I wish I'd never read this book. It's so awful." Well this has my attention now and I ask her if I could read it after she's finished. "You can have it", she said.

It was a true story about exorcism and a Lutheran Pastor named Rob (my husband's name) and his wife Carol (Rob's daughter's name). They successfully freed a woman inhabited by demon's. Well, now I must read this book. I read the book to Rob. We learned so much about evil and demons and how they enter a person's body and how to fend off an attack.

I did not know, after finishing the book, I would have an occasion to use what I learned. I was being prepared ahead of a forth coming situation. Again, God's perfect timing.

On a certain afternoon. I was in line to have lunch at the senior center. Coming up behind me was Nora Dee. She was shouting accusation's I couldn't relate to except one untrue remark that I told her was a lie and, "I don't have to do what you say and I don't have to do what you do", I said. She then shrieked, "Kiss my ass". I looked at her and questioned, "Child of God?" She shut down and left to return to join the friend whose business she was talking about.

We learned from Pastor Rob this is how a demon responds to the word. I would not have known this had I not read the book. These verbal accusations have been the reason and cause the friends have separated even when the attempt has been made to rectify any hurt feelings. The attempt was refused because, as my Vision pointed out, the Holy Spirit was left out.

What Vision? This Vision!

Here it is morning already, time to get up but where am I? I'm descending down stairs to a lower level. I'm in a bridal salon. There is a mannequin set up to be dressed for a bride's approval. I see a man, over there in the dark, waiting. I wondered why he was here. Oh! He's the groom, I realized.

Now I'm being moved behind the mannequin and the bride and here are the bride's maids. There is a glass partition between the bride and the bridesmaids. The bridesmaids are dressed in black lace with a small black lace veil on the back of their heads. They have no oil in their lamps.

Once again I'm moved where I join Rob and the bride. There's a problem with the head dress to be worn, either the white short veil on the back of the head, or the lovely brown velvet hat with a gorgeous live red rose was the choice. The hat kept sliding over the eyes of the mannequin and neither Rob nor I could make it stay as the bride watched. I said, "Here, let me do it". Well we were no help so we decided to leave.

We entered the elevator and turned to see That the bride had made her choice, which was the hat. In the elevator , along with us, floated the white veil. A bright beam of light from above filled the elevator.

Upon awaking, I knew the meaning to my vision and the answer's came. The bride was Johanna. The groom being kept in the dark is Rolf. The 5 bridesmaids having no oil in their lamps were not Spirit filled.

I was reminded of the bridesmaids in the Bible, whose lamps ran out of oil. They were not prepared. I recognized the bridesmaids. They were Johanna's friends, Nora Dee and Mona were trying To get Johanna's attention about the oil. The bridle veil was laced with tiny holes. A Holy Veil for a Holy Wedding. The beautiful hat is worn for a romantic wedding.

Here at this point in time is where we Leave the situation, the players and the choice.

Fatal Fall

On Dec, 26th, 2010 Ivey Mae, our cat, wants me to open the patio door so she can sniff the air outside thru the screen. Having just watered a plant, I have a glass of water in my hand but I go to open the door and return the glass to the kitchen. Enroute I trip over an exercise machine, fall forward and land on my chin on the wooden arm of a chair.

Bleeding profusely I call out to Rob, "Help me, help me." With no hesitation he helps me up and takes me to Emergency where after 3 hours and 16 stitches in my chin I return home.

The additive to this scenario is I no longer can sing, as I have been, which I have done since 8 years old in school, in church and in concert groups, etc. Now what can I do? This has been my service for receiving a singing voice from God. I go to choir rehearsal and find I can sing in the Tenor section but what do I sound like? Am I a help? I'm a high Soprano and think the sound in my head but now my sound comes from my chest.

Bemoaning my circumstance to God, "Now what can I do? This has been my responsibility, my commitment, etc.". My still small voice whispered, "Write a book!" "What would I name it?" I asked. "Tracking the Holy Spirit!" "I'll need an Author name. " He said, "Krystal Klear."

Mulling this over in my mind and In a conversation about my dilemma to a friend, she said, "Write a book." Write a book? Why would she think I could write a book? A second friend said the same thing. A third friend, a Christian Councilor said, "You write so well, why don't you write a book!" That did it. With pen in hand and lots of paper, I began. Not that I've been kept in the dark but I did not catch a typing error which left out a whole paragraph in this story, Fatal Fall. Another person, Melody was enlisted to point this out.

Shortly after my fall, Carolyn and John Haury located a specialist and two vocal trainers to help me. Carolyn is our choir director at St. Paul's Lutheran church in Dearborn. Such dedication! Such love! Such understanding. They'll get their wings for sure.

Melody was running me through my vocal exercises and between scale's, in conversation, we talked about my book. She would like to hear a story. I just happened to have it with me. I read to her, "Fatal Fall." She really liked how I write but suggested I add the three friends that I had eliminated. I'm unwilling to do this. I will only write what He says. However this suggestion did seem familiar so I got out my original copies and re-read the story. This is how I discovered the paragraph left out, through Melody's observation. It was included. There are those who would say, "Well, Elleen, it was meant to be." I agree.

Before leaving Melody asked what my favorite song is. I have so many but earlier that morning I had been casually tossing this and that out and rerouting stuff. That's when an out of place piece of music caught my eye. I love this melody! I love the words!

The Song:
While standing at the Cross (1)
by Frank L. Cross and Jane Carrier

The words:
While standing at the Cross what did I see?
I saw the eyes of Jesus looking down at me.
Amid the shadow's dim,
He bore my guilt deep and grim.
There my heart was drawn to him,
While standing at the Cross.

While standing at the Cross what did I do?
I felt my sin within me
piercing through and through.
My conscience burned in shame,
I had no one but me to blame.
In hope I called upon his name.
While standing at the Cross.

While standing at the Cross what did I say?
I cried, "Oh Lord, forgive me.
Take my sin away,"
And at the dreadful scene
He said, "My blood washed thee clean!"
Then I knew what love could mean.
While standing at the Cross.
While standing at the Cross.

I was so prepared to answer Melody's question with a song that gives us access to the Holy Spirit, as He promised.

You have read the messages of just a portion of my life's experiences so far which I would not have known or come to realize, had I not written this book. That all the while I was tracking the Holy Spirit He had been tracking me from the day of my baptism as an infant.

And the point is - - - - Krystal Klear

Primary Author The Holy Spirit

(1) MCMLXVI Lorenz Publishing Co. All rights reserved. Reproduced by permission.

www.ingramcontent.com/pod-product-compliance
Lightning Source LLC
Chambersburg PA
CBHW081022040426

42444CB00014B/3322